YOUR PERFECT LIFE

It's within your reach!

IO170146

Managing Editor:
Denny Portier-Terpstra

Contributors:
Barbara J. Cormack
Dr. Charuni Senanayake
Bettina Pickering
Loren Schmal

For more information: **www.Amarantine.life**

ISBN: (Print)   978-1-939556-39-4
ISBN: (eBook) 978-1-939556-40-0

ISSN: 2515-7434 (Online)
ISSN: 2515-7426 (Print)

First published: September, 2018 UK

Contents

Denny's Deliberations

by
Denny Portier-Terpstra

A Perfect Life...

Ever since I was a very small child, I have always dreamt of leading a life that was way better than my own. I have always longed for the nicer things in life; a bigger and better house, nicer toys, more beautiful surroundings, better weather, more money, nicer food and drinks, and so on. And as I grew into my teenage years, my dreams of that perfect life were expanded with dreaming of being very successful in my perfect career, finding and marrying that perfect gorgeous and loving husband, travelling to the most beautiful places on earth whilst staying in the most fantastic hotels with perfect service. And it wasn't just a dream, I knew with absolute certainty that life had all those bigger and better things in store for me.

But then, somewhere along the way; real life kicked in and disturbed those dreams. Reality taught me that there's nothing wrong with dreaming big, but that it can take a good while to achieve those big dreams. And in the meantime, life can actually be pretty tough! You'll need to study hard and start at the bottom of the career ladder, in order to eventually become great in any job. And that may take years. The first place where you will live on your own, will likely be tiny and rubbish, and if you're lucky enough you may be able to work your way up the property ladder over the years that follow. Taking a 5* first class trip around the world may be achievable, but it will take years and years of working and saving really hard to ever be able to a thing like that.

And as reality kicked in, almost automatically my dreams became much smaller and also much more realistic. I dreamed of living in a house, any house, instead of living in an apartment. I dreamed of getting a promotion at work, instead of aiming for that top-level-job straight away. I was very happy with my first ever 2* European island vacation, instead of longing for that 5* trip to Fiji.

But somewhere in the back of my mind, those old dreams must still have been alive. Because, when I think about them now and assess where I am today, I can see very clearly how my life has moved over the years towards that perfect life picture that I have created in my mind all those years ago. I'm not living my dream yet, but I have never been as close to doing so in my life before. And I can actually say that my life is pretty perfect as it is right now. And therefore I believe that, on a very unconscious level, those childhood dreams have guided me on my path. They helped me progress and keep moving forward, even when I didn't think about them.

If you want to live your perfect life too, then I hope this issue of Amarantine will inspire you on how to create your perfect life, and in the meantime, be grateful for what you have already achieved along the way.

Warmest regards,

Denny

Denny Portier-Terpstra
Managing Editor Amarantine

Your Life is

Your Life

your life is your life

don't let it be clubbed

into dank submission.

be on the watch.

there are ways out.

there is a light somewhere.

it may not be much light but

it beats the darkness.

be on the watch.

the gods will

offer you chances.

know them.

take them.

you can't beat death

but

you can beat death in life, sometimes.

and the more often

you learn to do it,

the more light there will be.

your life is your life.

know it while you have it.

you are marvellous

the gods wait to delight

in you.

The Laughing Heart
© Charles Bukowski

Today

is a perfect day

to start living

your dreams!

The Daily Quotes.com

8

Why can't you live your Perfect Life?

Forgiveness

It is not a virtue to suffer,
It is not a sin to be happy.
Paulo Coelho

It's often easier to continue to live the life that you are living today, to not rock the boat, or to put someone else or someone else's needs or wants before your own. By not wanting to rock the boat, or put your needs and wants first, you don't have to change or upset someone else's life, when you make the changes to your life that you want to make.

Are you sacrificing your own wants, needs, or well-being to make other people around you happy, or to avoid conflict?

Do you feel guilty when you consider your own needs, wants, or well-being first? Do you feel guilty when you consider setting boundaries to allow yourself some time and space for you? Does putting yourself first make you feel selfish? Does this selfish feeling bring guilt?

Often defining, creating, and living YOUR Perfect Life; does not mean that you are leaving others behind or moving away from others. It means that you are living the life you were meant to be living.

As part of defining your own Perfect Life, you can define boundaries to stop you from 'losing yourself'. These boundaries may be physical, emotional, or mental; and they will help you separate you, your feelings, your needs, your wants, your beliefs, your space, and your interests from those of others.

A physical boundary could be that you have a separate room in your home, which is your space and no-one else's, or it could be that you move into your own home or it could be that you move into a separate work or hobby environment. Emotional or mental boundaries are important so that you can express yourself without feeling that you need to take on someone else's emotions when you state your opinion. Boundaries simply create a separation between you and someone else.

Not allowing yourself to define and create your own Perfect Life means that you allow others to make your decisions for you; determine your environment; or even determine your health and well-being. You give and give without receiving anything in return. You run the risk of allowing yourself to be manipulated, used, and abused. You don't put any limits on how others can treat you. You don't stop others from expecting too much from you. You don't allow others to know that you have your own life to live.

It is hard to move from being someone who is living the life they are living today, to a position where they have defined, created, and are now living their own personally defined Perfect Life. The change or changes involved may mean that you leave a relationship/marriage, you move out of the home that you are now living in, move countries, change your employment position, stop providing finance for other people's desires and wishes, or a host of other things. One, some, more, all, or other changes may bring on a feeling of guilt.

Creating boundaries allows you to create your rules and exceptions in your relationships. Boundaries allow you and the others in your life to be clear about how to behave – what is acceptable behaviour and what is not acceptable behaviour. Boundaries are normal in relationships and they help you to identify your own identity and sense of self. If you don't define your boundaries, how do you know where they start and you end. Without boundaries, you will be behaving like a chameleon – always changing colours to suit someone else's wishes, desires, or requirements. Boundaries reduce the stress in your life. Defining and creating boundaries with you in mind, means that you are starting to take care of yourself. You are beginning to tell others what you want and need in your life, as well as demonstrating an understanding of what they need in their lives and how you fit in.

Bob Moawad said
"The best day of your life is the one
on which you decide your life is your own.
No apologies or excuses.
No one to lean on, rely on, or blame.
The gift is yours
- it is an amazing journey -
and you alone are responsible for the quality
of it.
This is the day your life really begins."

Ask yourself "why can't I live my own life?"

Accept, without question, that the best day of your life is the day you make the decision that your life is your own; that this is the day that your Perfect Life really begins. Recognise that when you accept that you can live your own life, that it is the day you start to define your Perfect Life and stop feeling guilty about everyone else.

Your Perfect Life?

Step-by-Step Series

by
Barbara J. Cormack

Perfect simply means 'having all the required or desired elements, qualities, or characteristics; as good as it is possible to be'; or 'absolute, complete'.

Over the past issues of Amarantine, you have become clear about where your life is today; you have identified the top three areas or segments of your life that you want to change; you have defined the reasons why you want to make these changes; you are clear about who wants you to make these changes (you or someone else); and now you'll start the process (one step at a time) to put these changes into place.

Before you start the process, take a few minutes to understand the big difference between WANTing and NEEDing. Often when you think about the changes you want to make to your life, these get confused. Yes, you NEED an income to be able to survive in today's world. Yes, you NEED a roof over your head. Yes, you NEED money to purchase food, drinks, and pay utility bills. No, you don't NEED a holiday. No, you don't NEED the best car money can buy. You may decide that you WANT a holiday for a very specific reason i.e. to take time out to focus on your health. You may decide that you WANT to buy the best car money can buy, but what would happen if you spent your income on that car and didn't have enough money to pay your utility bills, mortgage; or even put food on the table?

Defining your Perfect Life is about the things, people, environments, etc. that you WANT in your life; without forgetting that you still need to satisfy the NEEDs in your life.

When I left the UK and moved to the wonderful island of Madeira with my ex-husband, I went with a clear vision of what I THOUGHT life would be. Being born in the sub-tropics and having visited the island; the first time I landed at the airport, I felt I had 'come home'. It was this overwhelming emotion that gave me the feeling that I THOUGHT I wanted to live here. I didn't analyse the feeling, I just accepted it; and sometimes these emotions and feelings are absolutely accurate. Other times they are a small percentage accurate but don't consider your whole Wheel of Life; and that is what happened to me.

After finding a property that needed development, buying it, starting the development, selling the house in the UK, and moving; there were many experiences that gave me some clarity of what I WANTED from life. Yes, it was a fabulous environment – very spiritual, very friendly, very easy to live there; but …

After one particular experience, I moved out of our new home and into a studio apartment. At first my emotions went on a roller-coaster of a ride. One day I was convinced I was right; the next I was questioning my decision. I found a wonderful beach that allowed me the time and space to let my intuition guide my visualisations and explain what I WANTED in my life. After each visualisation meditation, I would return to my apartment and write down what I had seen in great depth. Every single detail I saw, would get written down.

Visualisations are simply a way of letting your minds-eye picture something. Although they can be used to picture happy or otherwise times in the past; they can also be used to create your vision of your future.

Sitting on the beach one day I realised that when I had felt 'at home' on the island of Madeira, I had not taken into account all the segments in my Wheel of Life. The feeling of returning 'home' was such a strong one, that it had overwhelmed everything else; and when my ex-husband had suggested that

15

we look for a property and purchase one, I had gone along with the flow. I was feeling very happy about returning to what felt like a European equivalent of my childhood, growing up in a third-world country in the sub-tropics.

Now, sitting on this beach I realised that I had not taken into consideration where my life was today; and clarified or identified what I wanted my life to be. I spent many hours over many days and weeks understanding my intuitive Perfect Life.

I had made the right decision. I was in the right place at this time.

Once I realised this, I followed the steps in the previous articles to become clear about what I wanted from my Perfect Life, and which three segments I should start working on first.

Now let's start working through the next step to successfully achieving your dream or aspiration.

1. Take the time to review your Wheel of Life, and the three segments you selected to focus on to make the changes to your life that you want to make.

2. Read the short sentences you wrote down to describe the end result (the dream/aspiration once you have successfully achieved it).

3. Think about your Perfect Life. Answering simply yes or no, does this dream/aspiration that you have selected give you the selected segment in your Perfect Life?

Your
Perfect Life?

If the answer is 'no' it is not a problem. Simply return to the article in Issue 2 about your Wheel of Life and follow through the exercises again. If the answer is 'yes', then continue through the next steps in this article.

Sometimes you will stop yourself from writing down the details of your Perfect Life; and there may be a valid reason for doing this.

A coaching article I read written by a client, talked about the decisions that they (the client) took when they worked through this process and were asked 'If you are defining your Perfect Life, will these goals help you live that life'? The client had to say 'no'. In discussing the reasons, the why, with their coach; the client realised that there was an intermediatory step that they had to complete. The step was to make sure that their children completed their high school education before the client left their spouse. As part of the discussions they had realised that they no longer wanted to remain in their marriage; but their sense of loyalty (and their inner values) would not allow them to disturb their children's education. This was important, as when the client started the next stage of their dream/aspiration achievement, they had to factor in the steps allowing them to stay in their marriage until the children had left home – a matter of 4 years!

This is the reason that I explain the WHY, for each change in your life will support you or not in making those changes. If the 'why' supports you in living the Perfect Life of your dreams, then you will achieve it. But often, if the 'why' highlights that the dream/aspiration is not your own but one that someone else wants you to achieve, you may not be successful.

There are examples all around us of how people do make

changes to their lives. Many years ago an advert in the UK highlighted that a simple memory can help make a change. I can never remember what the advert was advertising, but I do remember the story that was used. A young lady was driving to work through rush hour traffic with her thought bubble showing a gorilla. Remember that adverts are generally only 30 or 60 seconds long, so the very next picture showed the same young lady working with gorillas in the jungle. The advert doesn't show how she went from driving her car to work in rush hour traffic, to working in a jungle with the gorillas. What steps did she have to take? How long did it take her? But what it did highlight, was that she realised that there was a segment in her Wheel of Life that needed changing; and she took the steps to make that change.

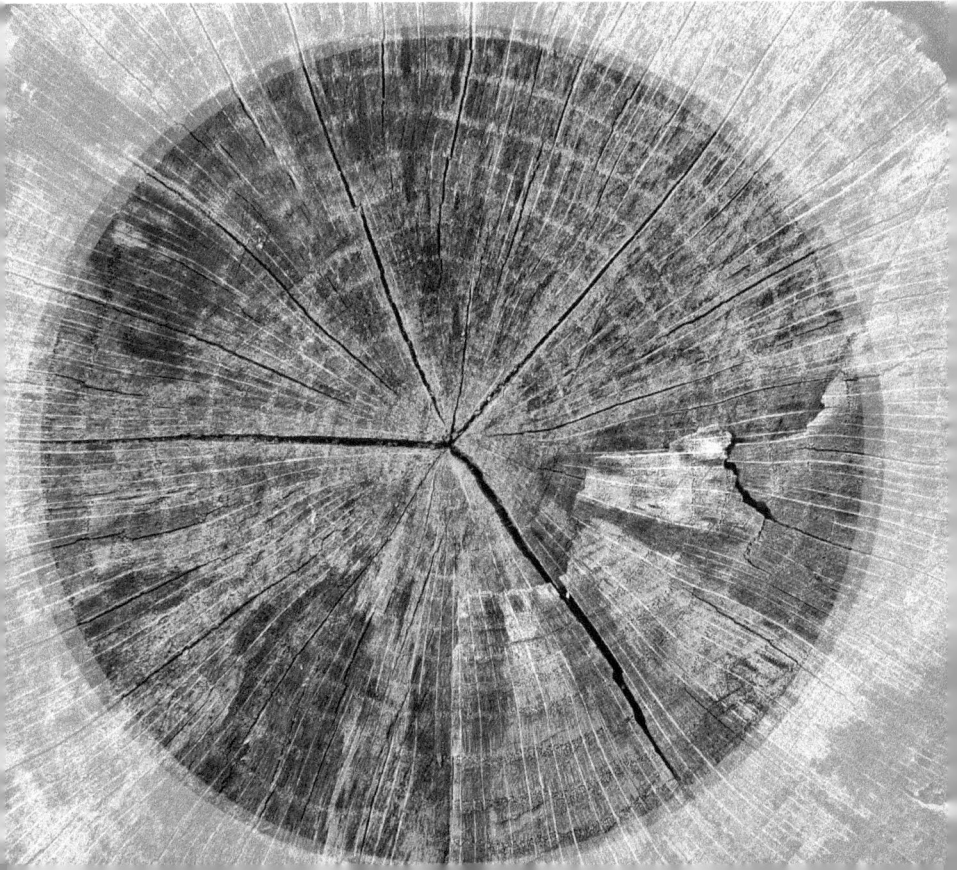

4. Now define your SMARTER goal(s)

    S   SPECIFIC
        It is important to be clear about what you want to achieve. For example, if you want to lose weight, knowing how many kilos you want to lose is specific. Saying 'I want to lose weight' is not specific; but 'I want to lose 10 kilos' is specific.

    M   MEASURABLE
        This definition will confirm whether you have or have not achieved your goal. Staying with the example of losing weight, 'I want to lose 10kilos' gives you the measure of 10 kilos. When you have achieved the 10 kilos of weight loss, that will confirm that you have successfully achieved your goal.

    A   AGREED, ATTAINABLE, ACHIEVABLE and ACTION-ORIENTED
        You are setting this goal, and now is the time to ask yourself 'do I want to achieve this goal?' If the answer is 'no', ask yourself what is not right. If it's a goal that has been 'given' to you i.e. your company goal to increase sales by 10%; you need to turn it around and work out how to make it your goal, so that you can agree with the goal. It is important that you AGREE with the SMARTER goal that you are setting, as statistics show that where you do not agree with the goal, you will not achieve it.
        Often you are asked if the goal is ATTAINABLE or ACHIEVABLE, but that is not the important question. I have talked in a previous issue about a presenter at a conference, talking about finding their 'dream' home and taking several house moves before they realised

that they had bought their 'dream' home. Another example was someone who wanted to be the 'next' President of the USA. For someone unknown, the coach questioned the word 'next'. The coach did not question the dream of being the President of the USA, but questioned the 'when' question of the word 'next'. Did the person become a President of the USA? Not yet, but is still working towards that goal.

ACTION-ORIENTED is something we will talk about later in this step. Goals are only achieved if you take the steps to achieve them.

R RELEVANT
You have taken your dream or aspiration and are now turning it into a SMARTER goal. Ask yourself 'is this goal relevant to the changes that I want to make to live my Perfect Life?

T TIMELY or TIME-BOUND
As a Spiritual Coach, I do find that this element can be a challenge, but it is important that you have an idea of when you want to complete your goal. For example, if you want to lose 10 kilos before you go on holiday; then the holiday start date is your deadline. If, like in the presentation that I attended, you want to live in a specific house, there may be a number of smaller goals to achieve before you achieve your final goal. It is important to define your BIG goal that meets the Perfect Life definition you have created.

E EXCITING or EXCITED
Any goal that you want to achieve must be one that you live and breathe every minute of every day. When

you think about it, it must bring a smile to your face and make you feel happy and cheerful. When you visualise yourself in your end result, you must in your inner most heart know that your Perfect Life will be a happy and exciting life.

R   RECORDED

Statistics show that those people who WRITE down their goals are successful. Writing them down gives you the opportunity to read them every day. Reading them gives you the chance to stay focused.

WRITE down your goal in a short and focused sentence, including every element of the important information that you have collated; starting with 'Today, the 'end result date' I am 'specific/measurable'. For example, today is the day I go on holiday (15th October, 2018) and I am ... kilos (10kgs less than you are today) in weight'.

5. Ask yourself 'does this goal meet my Perfect Life dream/aspiration visualisation'?

   If you answer is 'yes', then you know that what you have defined is absolutely what you WANT in your life. If you answer is 'no', go back to your Wheel of Life.

Often you define your Perfect Life based on your current situation. When you define your Wheel of Life, you think about the segments of your life as they are today. You don't always think about what segments are missing from your Wheel of Life. When you are rating your life, you rate it based on your current situation.

What would happen if you were to do the exercise again and create your Perfect Life Wheel of Life?

Taking this step with a client many years ago, highlighted that the client had defined their Wheel of Life based on their current situation. When they worked through the SMARTER exercise, they realised that they had selected to live the life that suited the other people in their life. When we talked about defining a Wheel of Life that suited their intuitive meditative visualisation, it highlighted the differences.

The initial Wheel of Life segments are not wrong and the goals defined based on that initial Wheel of Life may still be valid. What this second Perfect Life Wheel of Life highlights is that there may be other things that you need to consider.

Once you have defined your goals through writing down each dream/aspiration using the SMARTER process, you can start working on achieving your goals.

Barbara J. Cormack

© 2018 Barbara J. Cormack

Barbara J. Cormack AFC, AFM, MNMC is an award winning coach, an author, mentor, trainer, and a sought after international speaker.

People try to create
an outwardly perfect life,
but the quality of life
is based on the inward.
Jaggi Vasudev

Live life
to the fullest,
and
focus on
the positive.
Matt Cameron

Shoot for the Moon.
Even if you miss,
you'll land among
the stars.
Les Brown

**Very little is needed
to make a happy life;
it is all within yourself,
in your way of thinking.**
Marcus Aurelius

**Only I can
change my life.
No-one
can do it for me.**
Carol Burnett

**Far better to live
your own path imperfectly,
than to live another's perfectly.**
Bhagavad Gita

We must let go

of the life we have planned,

so as to accept

the one that is waiting for

us.

Joseph Campbell

Top Tips

To live Your Perfect Life!

"Your time is limited,
don't waste it living someone else's life.
Don't be trapped by dogma,
which is living
the result of other people's thinking.
Don't let the noise of other's opinion
drown your own inner voice.
And most important,
have the courage to follow
your heart and intuition,
they somehow already know
what you truly want to become.
Everything else is secondary."
Steve Jobs

It is often thought that you cannot live a Perfect Life, but who says that you cannot? There is no definition of a Perfect Life, other than the one that you create. These top tips will help you create the vision of your Perfect Life.

1. **Whose life are you living?**
   It is very easy as your adult life gets more involved with other people and other responsibilities, to lose track of the dreams that you had. Doing your own Wheel of Life will allow you to (1) identify the segments of your life as it is today, (2) clarify how you feel about each segment, and then add a further step (3) to identify what is missing from your life. What have you given up for other people, other commitments, or other responsibilities? Identifying what is missing, doesn't always mean that you want to include these elements in your life; but it does give you the option to answer the question 'whose life are you living?'

2. **What do you want your life to look like?**
   Take yourself forward in your life, about five years, and in your mind's eye, see your life in pictures. Let your imagination run wild, allow your intuition to share, and **see** yourself in your future; **hear** what is being said around you, to you, and what you are saying; look around and **see** where you are – what does the environment look like; **who** is with you; what **colours** are around you; what **aromas** can you smell; and **feel** how you are feeling. Run this movie in your mind, making tweaks, until you are clear that this is the life you would like to live.

3. **Perfect Wheel of Life**
   Taking the details from your visualisation of what you want your life to look like, create your Wheel of Life with all the relevant segments.

4. **Eliminate the unnecessary**
   If you really want to live your own life, it is important that you identify those elements of your current life that is/are preventing you from living the life of your dreams. These elements may be people, habits, thoughts, career, events, and so on. Identify each element that does not have a place in your perfect life.

5. **Find your passion**
   It is very easy to find your passion. It's something that you've kept hidden for many years. Take yourself back to when you were 5 or 6 years old and someone asked you 'what you wanted to be, when you grew up'. What did you say? What did you think?

   Many years ago I was talking to a client and she shared her childhood dream with me – she wanted to be a teacher; primary school teacher. Her father immediately said 'no, you need to get a proper job'. His idea of a 'proper job' was one that was tied to earning a high level of income – solicitor, accountant, and anything similar. The scary thing was that I heard my father saying the same thing to me, all those years ago. Unlike the times gone by, today you can live the life of your dreams. You do not have to 'fit in' with someone else's idea, 'comply' with someone else's image of your life. Stop! Write down your passion.

6. **Habits, Thoughts, Ideas**
   What habits have you got that need to change?

   What do you do when you have a negative thought?

   What happens when you have an idea that would allow you to fulfil your passion?

   Often this is where you need to start to make those changes that will allow you to live the life of your dreams, the life of your passion. What do you need to do to have positive habits, positive thoughts, and are never stopped when you have an idea that allows you to fulfil your passion?

7. **How can you make your passion earn your income?**
   You are encouraged to have a 'job', to build a 'career', and often this comes from something of interest, or good school results; but what type of life would you live if you could earn your income from doing something that you are passionate about?

   It's easy to say 'I can't do this', but what if you took some time out right now and investigated how you could earn your income from your passion? An advert many years ago confirmed this. It showed a girl in her mid-20's, stuck in her car in a traffic jam. The traditional 'bubble thought' was of orangutans. She saw herself cuddling them. Adverts are quick, so the next picture you see is her being instructed in her new job – looking after a family of orangutans in Borneo. Wow! What's stopping you?

8. **What else?**
Traditional jobs generally take $1/3^{rd}$ of your week, working Monday to Friday between 9am and 5pm; but if you want to do other things with your life, then being clear about how much time you need to earn your income, will allow you to incorporate the 'what else'. Hobbies are important. These are other areas of interest to you and should be important enough to be included in your perfect life. For some people this maybe photography, whereas for others it may be rebuilding a classic car. Whatever else you want in your life, find a way to include it.

9. **Who?**
It's natural to want other people in your life. Now is your opportunity to be clear about who they might be.
Significant Other. Children. Parents. Grandchildren.
Close friends. Best friend/Confidant.
Colleagues. Acquaintances. Everyone else.

People come, and people go! Some people are designed to come into your life and stay. Others are designed to come into your life for a reason; which may be to help you learn a lesson, or it may be to support them learning a lesson. It's important to be clear about who you want in your life permanently, as well as who has come in and will go out when the time is right.

10. Where?

Are you living and working in the right place in the world? You may own a house, be paying a mortgage, be settled into a community; but if your perfect life needs you to be living somewhere else – where is that?

One of the presenters in a course I attended many years ago explained that he knew that he and his wife (and children) were living in the wrong house. He had seen a picture of the house he wanted to live in – not only the house but also the environment. He cut out the picture and put it on his vision board. They packed up the house and moved. The vision board got rolled up and put into a cardboard storage box. Several house moves later, they decided that need to clear all the 'stuff' that had moved with them over the various house moves. Imagine his surprise, when he pulled out his vision board and found that they had just moved into the house of his dreams.

11. Explore!

Saying 'yes' to opportunities allows you to explore and experiment; both of which are important in allowing you to define, create and live your perfect life. The world changes on a daily basis, and it's important that you keep up with those changes.

12. Give!

Giving is the best investment you can make in defining, creating, and living your perfect life. Everyone has a tendency to 'buy' and one of the easiest ways to start the 'giving' process is to recycle – give away what you don't need or want in your closet / wardrobe / home / office / etc. In other words, declutter. Another way of giving is to volunteer to a charity – it may be one that means you need to go to the charity or it may be one that needs time, which you can give from home. Giving brings a lightness into your life. The space you create around you allows you to determine and define what you truly want in your perfect life.

13. **Be grateful**

Be thankful for what you have. Be thankful for what you can have. Be thankful that you have the time and opportunity to define, create, and live your perfect life. Be grateful for each step of your journey, from where you are in your life today, to actually living your perfect life.

Changing your life from where it is today to living your perfect life will take time. It is not impossible to live your perfect life, and somewhere along the path you may forget that you can - if you chose to - live your perfect life. One step, or an event, or something may stop you. Be grateful for that opportunity to reflect on what you've done, what you've got, where you are, and who you are with.

To keep yourself moving forward, one step at a time, when you define your life; create a burning desire in your definition. One that will keep the flame burning, the willingness in you to sacrifice what you need to let go of, the patience to take one step at a time, and a strong belief that you can life your perfect life.

One day you will realise that you've achieved your goal. You have come to the end of this particular path and your journey has come to an end. Be grateful for all that you've learnt along the way. Then go out and CELEBRATE! with gratitude the life you are now living – YOUR PERFECT LIFE!

Is Your Perfect Life, a Peaceful one?

by

Dr Charuni Senanayake

Am I living the life of my dreams?

In short my view of perfection of life equals to peacefulness of life. We all have dreams, goals, targets, and as we go on achieving them, do we feel a peacefulness within us? When I look at my life from this angle, it naturally becomes a great discovery.

My own reflection of my life is as below.

> I studied in local school in Sri Lanka. I couldn't get to the medical college in my country, as I was short of 5 marks, so that made me apply for scholarships in China for Medicine. During my last year in China, as I was an intern doctor, China was hit by Severe Acute Respiratory Disease (SARS) and I experienced the effect and impact of epidemics on public health first hand. I pursued a Masters in the UK in Public Health, and because of the interest that I had now developed in Public Health. After that, I looked for a job in an International Non-Governmental Organization, and I found one with the World Health Organization and worked in that job for over 10 years. Then I moved on, back to Sri Lanka, to let my children grow up in my culture as they were still young. I set up a partner organization of the International Academy of Mentoring and Coaching (IAMCasia) and gave back to my motherland by providing them with the opportunity to learn about Coaching and Mentoring, turn around businesses and teach skills and techniques for bringing out the best in people and teams. I also work part time for a hospital chain in wellness, where I help people be healthy, identify risk factors and motivate them to take responsibility for their health. Today, I love doing what I am doing, and I feel happy and peaceful deep inside.

Does this mean that I don't have future goals? Of course not! In fact, I have massive plans!

Amidst all this, how did I manage to have a peaceful life?

Find inner peace within your self

Reflection is a great way to find peace in your life. Reflect on life's most difficult situations and decisions, and come to terms with why you did what you did at that time. There are no right or wrong ways; you have done what you had to do and could do under the circumstances presented at that time.

Once the circumstances have changed, and you reflect on why you've reacted the way that you did, it's easy to get caught by remorse. But that's unfair to yourself, as you have learned from your experience, and are wiser today because you have passed the circumstances that you faced earlier. There is no point in thinking how you could have done things differently, of you are measuring your actions at the time against the knowledge that you have gained in the process.

When I am feeling deeply upset, or feeling a shift of balance in my life, I book an appointment with myself for reflection time, to examine my thoughts in a beautiful and quiet place. My favorite place has always been the sea side, where I can see blue everywhere, calming my soul, thoughts and clearing my head of clutter, so that I can actually look behind the emotions of what I am feeling, why I am feeling the way that I do, and take decision about what I should actually be doing.

When you are angry; deal with it

When you are angry, find a quiet place where you can take a few deep breaths. Go out and go for a walk, listen to some

soft music, etc. Get the rising emotions under control and think about how to deal with the situation at hand.

Revisit the situation with a clear mind. Not only would you be able to see things as they are, but it will also become easier to find a long lasting solution and answers that won't lead to any hurt or regret later on.

Don't be afraid to move on

One of the best qualities I feel that I have, is my ability to move on, rather than to keep on sulking for long periods of time when things didn't go exactly as I planned. This sometimes makes the people closest to me wonder how I can do that, without giving things a second look or thought. Every single time that I have failed to do what I had attempted to do, I have regarded that as practice; an experience. This allows me to put it quickly behind me, and refocus my energy again on the next step forward. Some people therefore think that I am too optimistic and never think about my mistakes, and they wonder how I can learn from them. But what they don't realise, is that instead I am just very quick to admit my mistakes, analyse them, and promise myself never to repeat them. So learning from them is easy for me, and usually much faster achieved then others can. And above all, I'm reluctant to waste my life thinking about things which I cannot change because they happened in the past.

See the good in everything

When you look at life from the brighter side, most of the time it gets easier to live it. Of course, not all things which look good are innocent or are there for your best interest. However, live becomes easier to live if you chose optimism over suspicion. I really love the quote below, which captures this view perfectly:

*"Any day above ground is a good day.
Before you complain about anything,
be thankful for your life
and the things that are still going well."*
Germany Kent

This quote is a stark reminder for us to appreciate the things around us, people around us and to see good in everything around us.

Learn to forgive easily

*"Today I decide to forgive you,
not because you apologized or
because you acknowledged the pain
that you've caused me,
but because my soul deserves peace."*
Najwa Zebian

Inner peace is very important to us as human beings, and even more so in our world today as it is changing so quickly with technical advancement leading to us becoming more isolated. It's much better to be happy with the family and friends and other people that are important to us, then to waste our time thinking about people or circumstances that remind of bitterness and bad memories. When you decide to love and let go of hurt, forgiveness automatically happens. When relationships break down, people initially go to extra mile to blame themselves for the failure of the relationship. Then, your mind will start to gather evidence that the other person hurt you, and slowly the bitterness turns into anger or even hatred. It boils in our insides every single day, blocking all our pathways to happiness and peace. Learn to choose love over hatred; choose happiness over pain. Learn to focus on the people that make you happy, instead of on those who have hurt you deeply. Learn to leave, rather than sticking around with pain. Know that everything is temporary, and so will be your pain.

Be the change you want to see in the world

Your external world is created by the inner reality of yourself. So as human beings, we have a 'non-physical' consciousness, which creates and demonstrates as 'physical'. Consciousness in its form creates vibrations which are pure and positive. The physical form of us catches these vibrations, and does everything to manifest them.

If you want to create a perfect peaceful life, look deeply into yourself, look for conflicting ideas buried deep inside you, be the change first within and bring yourself to be aligned with who you are. Let go of any fear-based thoughts holding you back. Start listening to your heart, stop being influenced by the negative 'tape recorder' inside your head. Just align your inner self to be in peace with your total self, and you will see the outside reality will match up to what you really are inside.

Charuni Senanayake
© 2018 Dr Charuni Senanayake

Life Coach,
Executive Coach
and
Coach Trainer

When is Life actually perfect?

Research

If people could choose their ideal life, what level of happiness, pleasure, freedom, health, self-esteem, longevity and intelligence would they aspire to achieve?

This interesting question was central to a global study - carried out across 8000 participants from 27 countries - by an international team of psychologists, and with the results published in "Psychological Science" in June 2018.

For decades, if not for centuries, especially in the Western World it has been believed that people strive to achieve the very best that life has on offer for them. And when you look at our society today, and how we go about life, this belief has been fully embedded in most aspects of everyday life. From a young age onwards, we are thought that we should always give our very best in anything we do, in our to achieve maximum results. We need to train and practice hard for our sports, so that we or our team can become the best at their level. We need to study hard in school, so that we can ultimately complete the highest possible level of education. We need to work hard for our professional and career development, in order to climb the career ladder and land the best possible job. And all of that is being done with the explicit promise of greater recognition and better rewards at the end of the line.

But how can it be that some people seem to "sabotage" themselves? People who have every opportunity to achieve success in one or more areas of their lives, and who simple choose not to actively pursuit those opportunities. People who can achieve the very best that life has to offer, and who simply just settle for less? Why aren't they motivated by, and striving for, that greater recognition and those better rewards?

The answer to these questions was found in the research: people are actually rather modest in their desires to achieve perfection in life, and on average they only strive to achieve 70-80% of "perfection". The research also showed that people were even more moderate in their desires, when they come from countries that have traditions based on Buddhism or Confucianism.

In the press release about this research, co-author Dr Paul Bain from the Department of Psychology of the University of Bath explains: *"We're often told we have unlimited wants and that we should strive for self-betterment in all that we do. But we can't satisfy every want, suggesting we should be constantly frustrated, always compromising. Whilst this may be true for some people, our research suggests that these people are in the minority. Instead, our research suggests that most people have limited wants. For the majority of us, 'the perfect, or ideal world' is fairly modest. We don't aspire to be the richest or smartest in the world, and not even necessarily to have perfect health."* And lead author, Dr Matthew Horney of the University of Queensland, adds: *"People want positive qualities, such as health and happiness, but not to the exclusion of other darker experiences".*

http://journals.sagepub.com/doi/pdf/10.1177/0956797618768058
http://www.bath.ac.uk/announcements/study-points-to-a-moderate-version-of-the-perfect-life/

Life is not always perfect

but it's what you make it.

So make it count,

make it memorable,

and never let anyone steal

your happiness.

CatchSmile.com

Role Models?

Newest Trends

VICTORIA·R·I·

A role model is simply someone who you aspire to be. There may be one aspect of their live you would like to emulate in yours or many.

When thinking about your Perfect Life, which aspect of your role model(s) life would you like to incorporate into your life? Most people have one or more role models in their life; a parent, a friend, a teacher, a headmaster/mistress, a sports hero, someone you have read about or seen on TV or the internet, someone whose book you've read or read about in a book, someone whose course you've followed, or anyone who has something in their life you aspire to have in yours.

Although a generic definition of a role model is that it is simply someone who you aspire to be, it's difficult to truly define a role model. Everyone has a different reason for having a role model. Traditionally, a role model has been someone older, but with the millennial generation (also known as Generation Y) your role model may be someone younger than you.

Although most people are unable to have their role model as their mentor, it does not stop you from using your aspiration to include one or more aspects of their life into your definition of your Perfect Life.

When you look at someone like Richard Branson, who happily does not wear a business suit for business reasons, you may aspire to be able to 'go to work' wearing whatever you want to wear and not conform to what is expected that you will wear. Oprah Winfrey may be a role model because of her compassion or her status as a thought leader. Prince William has stated that the Queen is one of his greatest role models, she is his inspiration. Michelle Obama is a role model for many; she is a hard worker who fights for what she believes in. Malala Yousufzai is a role model followed by many females who have not been allowed education. Kate Middleton - or to give her her full title; Catherine, Duchess of Cambridge - is a role model for showing reserved, graceful and proper behaviour; yet doesn't flaunt her position in life today. Mother Teresa is known to be a role model for her caring, selfless, religious and risk taking personality.

From birth you have been learning from others – how to walk, how to talk, how to hold a conversation, how to eat, how to think, and how to behave. During these formative years of your life, you have watched and learnt from others (parents, older siblings, grandparents, aunts, uncles, cousins, neighbours, friends, teachers, etc.). You have aspired to be the same or similar to these other people for one or more reasons.

So from childhood, children look at others, regardless of whether that other person is a good influence or not, to aspire to what they want in life. This is not an activity that you start after you've left school... it's something that you've been doing naturally all your life.

Now is a time to consciously look at those around you and identify how someone else can help you define one element of your Perfect Life.

Many years ago I attended a Bootcamp and one of the presenters was talking about Mood Boards and their benefit. He explained that he knew someone (one of his role models) who was living in the house of his own dreams. An architectural magazine did a full article on the house: the location, each room, the outlook from each room; the way in which the room was used; the reason for selecting the colours; and the article went on into much more detail. The

presenter explained that he cut out the images and put these on his Mood Board – his Perfect Life House. He cut out the article and wrote the changes he would make, in the columns i.e. colour of rooms, furniture selection. He put the updated article on his Mood Board. For many years he had the Mood Board in his study and he saw – consciously looking at it, or unconsciously just being aware of it – this board every day. Some days he would study the Mood Board and if something didn't look quite right, he would make changes. Other days he would just be aware that it was there.

He and his family outgrew their house. He and his wife put their current house on the market and started to pack up 'non-essentials'. The Mood Board was a 'non-essential', so it got rolled up and stored into a cardboard storage tube; ready to be moved to the new house. Moving day arrived and everything got moved from their current house to their new house. As they were unpacking items for each room, they agreed that the 'non-essential' items could be packed at a later date. Right now it was important for them to unpack the essentials for each room.

Another house move and the essentials and non-essential items got moved. Some of these non-essential items were still packed from their first move – the Mood Board was in this category.

Two or three moves later, they moved into a new house and decided that every single box would be unpacked and a decision would be made about the contents. As previously, they unpacked the essentials. They created a home they wanted to live in. Unlike previous moves, they had not put the non-essential boxes into a garage, but had kept them in the house for a 'rainy day'. The 'rainy day' arrived and they started to unpack each box and make a decision – did it stay or did it go? As they hadn't used a number of the items originally packed before their first move, they went. He picked up the cardboard storage tube and pulled out the Mood Board. Opening it up and laying it out on a table, both he and his wife stopped in surprise.

He had been extremely clear about the environment he wanted to live in – his Perfect Life house. His wife had agreed with him, and they had agreed that this was the house of their dreams.

Their surprise ... they had just bought this house!

A bigger surprise! As he read the article and his notes, they realised that each room was as he had stated – colour, furniture choice, etc.

Their success in creating, moving into and living their Perfect Life, was that for this aspect, they had clearly defined each element of their home in their Perfect Life.

Remembering that you can have many role models; all for different reasons: which role model will you aspire to be in defining each aspect of your Perfect Life?

My imperfectly perfect life!

by
Bettina Pickering

I still remember it vividly. That afternoon as I stood bewildered among all crowd of German carnival revellers holding, onto my grandfather's hand. All around me there was mayhem. People on artistically designed floats in colourful costumes throwing sweets into the cheering crowd. I did not understand the themes of the floats. I could not connect with the crowd, their accent and why they were so intensely trying to have fun, kiss each other and use any excuse to grope.

It did not feel like fun to me.

I felt like an alien.

In that moment, I took a decision:

I needed to leave Germany and live in a country where people were more like me. At the time, I called them 'normal people', well normal for me anyway.

I was 5 years old.

At that time, I did not understand my Meyers-Briggs preferences, my DISC profile, nor had I heard of the NLP metaprogrammes[1]. I just felt out of place, out of time, alien and misunderstood.

My natural reactions where not seen as normal amongst my Kindergarten peers, in primary or in secondary school. Only when I was on holiday in Ireland, did I feel, I was amongst

---

[1] All of these assessments offer different perspectives on behavioural preferences, i.e. when an event happens what behaviour do we go to first or instinctively e.g. are we more proactive or reactive, do we seek our energy from outside or inside ourselves and so on.

'normal' people. I had the same feeling when I went to England.

Much later in life, when I was working in a global consultancy and had the opportunity to do my MBTI profile, the aha I got from reading my profile felt like an explosion of fireworks.

When I was about 15, I had another vision of my perfect life. I wanted to be a wife to either a farmer or someone with a business, who I could support and have a lot of children with. We would have animals and live in the country. I never wanted to study, to write a book or even to go to university or get a degree.

What is interesting, my resolution at 5 years old came true. I left Germany, settled in the UK and am now starting to establish a base in Ireland.

My dream at 15 - the husband, the children and shared business - never materialised. I got married and divorced, met someone else who was a soul mate fit but did not want children, whilst they were open to share a business.

Instead, I attracted animals in need of support, attracted a wonderfully diverse and inspiring circle of friends, learnt Qi Gong and became a Qi Gong teacher, became a Master Coach and Master Mentor, did three masters' degrees (I always have to laugh at that one – the person who at 15 did not want to study!!), spent 13 years in global transformation and change management consulting, have been running a successful business from the UK for 8 years and just set up my business in Ireland. And, there is so much more.

Do I regret my life, what I did and what I did not do? **No**.

Do I sometimes wish that my dream at 15 years old had come true? **Yes, of course I do. And, I also know that that dream may not have kept me satisfied for long.**

"I love my life
not because it is full of perfect experiences,
but because I solely owe myself
unconditional self-love in abundance.
So what would be your excuse
not to love your life unconditionally?"
Edmond Mbiaka

Life is not perfect

One thing I learnt, is that life is full of surprises, twists and turns. It leads us to what we need to explore or learn the most. Sometimes the lessons are hard, sometimes they feel perfect and sometimes they cannot be topped.

Striving for perfection is exhausting. More often than not, the never-ending quest for perfection leads to unhappiness and dissatisfaction.

If you don't love your life, you have a choice

Most people I have come across are unhappy with their life at some point, or at several points or stretches, of their lives.

Some people never shift from those points. They feel perpetually unhappy or dissatisfied. Others experience ups and downs. Or they are unhappy with parts of their life, and happy with the other parts.

Now, the great thing is, if you are unhappy with something,

you can make a change. You have choices, even if these choices at that moment in time do not seem feasible or realistic. They are there, just waiting for you to notice them.

Dream big, start small

If you are unhappy with your life or part of your life, I would not advocate to search for your life purpose that very minute. It is certainly an option, however a lot of my clients found that starting a search for their life purpose is highly frustrating and disappointing, as they were not even clear what made them unhappy and what they truly wanted from life.

One amazing principle I leant from my Qi Gong teachers, is that Qi (i.e. energy) is waiting for you. The same with dreams and purpose. These are already created for you, and they wait for you to be ready to notice them. If we chase energy, it becomes elusive. If we try to grasp after it and try to contain it, again it evaporates and disappears. We need to create the space so that Qi, the dream, the purpose, can reveal itself to us.

Do dream big if you already have dreams or the inkling of a dream. Do develop that. It will give you the motivation, momentum and energy to change. However, enjoy the dream fully, rather than comparing your current life to the dream. Comparing is chasing, so the dream will become elusive.

If you start big, i.e. trying to close the gap between your dream and your current life, you are constantly reminding yourself of the gap. This enhances what negative emotions you experience about your life and tends to keep you stuck. Your brain tends to focus on the unhappiness, the past and the gap, instead of the possibility and the future.

Here is how to start:

1. **Make an agreement with yourself.**
   Adopt a mindset of:
   - this is a journey,
   - it takes as long as it takes,
   - there is no pressure,
   - when you are ready, the answer will reveal itself,
   - you are unique and thus there is no comparison to others, and
   - everything is possible.

   You might need to write this down and remind yourself of these statements daily.

   Why?

   Studies have shown that what we tell ourselves we become, what we expect, is what we attract. So, let's change that mindset to attract possibility instead of what you don't what.

2. **Focus on your needs.**
   Do a very simple practice every day whenever you feel unhappy or dissatisfied:
   - Identify the feeling – name it clearly (it might be several emotions or feelings),
   - Identify what you need right now – name it clearly (again there might be several needs),
   - Identify at least one action that you can take that will address at least one need that day (make sure that all actions can be initiated by you, and don't rely on others taking the initiative. Actions can include making a request, for example),

- o Carry out the action.

Why?

Satisfying your deepest needs first will release the unhappy feelings and create space for possibility, creativity and power. Each action you take, will take you closer to happiness.

To help you with this you can download my free Connect with your Emotions process from www.bettinapickering.com/resources/gifts.

3. **Understand how you are interacting with your life.**
   Treat it as if it was a person, a friend or relative.
   - o What is your relationship with your life?
     Do you go with the flow? Do you ask for what you need? Do you give back? Do you share your life? Do you give thanks for what life gives you? Do you notice your life? Are you present to it? Take a few minutes to assess how you interact with life and your life.
   - o What do you notice about your relationship with life?
   - o What possibilities for change do you notice?
   - o Identify one action where you can change your relationship with life today.

Why?

We often just drift through life rather than being an proactive participant. We accept unconsciously that it will be as it is because of upbringing, role models such as parents, culture and/or fear of the unknown. By understanding our relationship with life currently, we can change it. Again, go for small changes. These are exponential and will lead to much bigger transformation.

Cycle through these steps a few times, before going back to your dream (or dreams, or quest for purpose) and identify what steps or questions might belong on a roadmap that will help you get there.

In all of this, acknowledge your achievements and your journey to who you are now. Don't dismiss it. It is really important to appreciate yourself and how far you have come, no matter your age or circumstances.

This will help you shift from being a passenger in your life, to the driver of your life. It will help you build a strong foundation to weave your dream into reality and/or meet your purpose.

Bettina Pickering

© 2018 Bettina Pickering

Bettina Pickering is a transformative leadership coach, entrepreneur mentor, business transformation and change consultant, author and speaker.

What is a Perfect Life?

Self-Care

"I have a perfect life where I read;
I go out into the wilderness and camp.
I meet scientists and learn about their studies
of wild animals,
and then I come home...
and start creating the world I have seen."
Jean Craighead George
(American Writer, 1919 – 2012)

What is a perfect life? Is it a life that can be described as 'entirely without any flaws, defects, or shortcomings'? Probably not. More probably it's a life that has everything in it, and everyone in it, that you aspire to having as part of your Perfect Life.

Madelaine Petsch said "There is no perfect life. There is always something going on behind the curtain that people don't know about." and she is right. Day-to-day living and day-to-day decisions may highlight the flaws, defects, and shortcomings in your everyday life, but this does not need to stop you from defining, creating, moving into, and living your Perfect Life, one step at a time.

Your Perfect Life will have all the things that you want to do, all the activities that you want to spend your time on doing, living in the environment you want to live in, and all the people you want to be living with, socialising with, working with, and communicating with.

"Death is not the greatest loss in life.
The greatest loss is
what dies inside us while we live."
Norman Cousins

Whether you are or are not familiar with the Wheel of Life, it's one of the tools used by coaches to help you understand each element, each part, or each segment of your life. Although the full method for using the Wheel of Life is found in Issue 1 of Amarantine Magazine, in this issue we'll focus on using the Wheel of Life to create YOUR PERFECT LIFE!

Often a Wheel of Life denotes all the areas of your life that you think should be there, but today we won't be focusing on what should be there, but on what would make your Perfect Life if it were there.

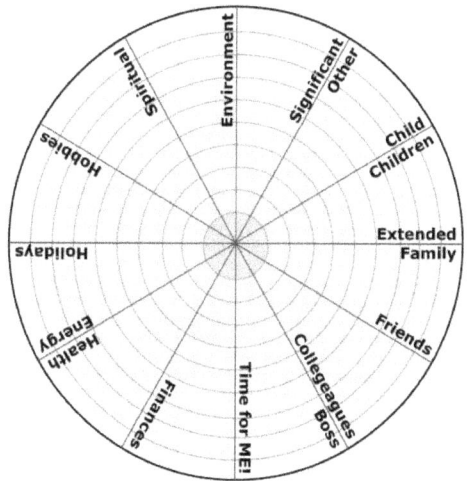

This Wheel of Life is taken from a standard coaching Wheel of Life and incorporates everything that you and/or your coach feels should be included in your life today. This type of Wheel of Life will allow you to determine how balanced your life is today and for that reason it is a very valuable tool.

Thinking specifically about your perfect life, look at a differently completed Wheel of Life; one in which you can start to determine what your Perfect Life will look like. The type of life you dream about. The life you aspire to be living.

Although for your Perfect Life it is easy to visualise what your life will be like; a visualisation exercise will create one perfect day or one perfect moment, whereas using the Wheel of Perfect Life will allow you to determine each element of your perfect life in detail.

We have created a Wheel of Perfect Life with 12 elements, but when you are defining your own you can create as many or as few elements as you wish.

To do this exercise you will need a clean and fresh journal. A journal is simply book, an app on your mobile, pieces of paper; that come together to create your thoughts, ideas, questions, concerns, fears, and intuition. It is not something that captures your daily activities (that is a diary); it is free flowing with no set or specific dates or sections.

Before you continue with this exercise, clear your mind of all your current thoughts – work, spouse/partner, children, friends, customers, or anything else. Turn off your mobile! Make sure that any other method of communication is closed down. Let those around you know that you need time with no disturbances or interruptions to work through this process. It is important that you have no interruptions while you work on your own Perfect Life.

STEP ONE

Write down all the areas of which you dream of including them in your Perfect Life. There may be some that you dream you wish to include, but you don't feel are realistic; today is not about logic or practicality; today is about your dreams and aspirations.

STEP TWO

There is no right and there is no wrong to the number of segments you have in your life, although I would caution you to group like elements together e.g. 'health' could incorporate 'physical fitness', 'fitness', 'optimum health'. Once you have your list, look through it, and see how many of your segments are similar and group them together.

STEP THREE

Now draw yourself a circle with the right number of segments to allow you to put one element into each segment. For later use, it would be beneficial to create one with 10 rings.

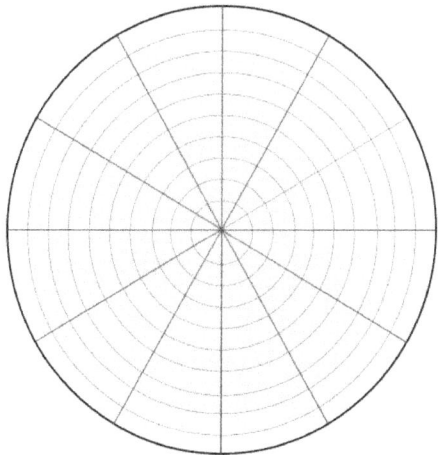

STEP FOUR

Once you have drawn your Wheel of Life, enter onto it all your OWN elements that defined your perfect life.

Areas not covered in our Wheel of Perfect Life example include Personal Development, Professional Development, Education, Learning, and a range of other topics. This Wheel of Perfect Life is an example of what can be included in your Wheel. It's important, when you are creating your own Wheel of Perfect Life, that you create the elements that you want in your life; not the elements that you 'feel' you 'should' have; and not the elements someone else tells you to have. This is your Perfect Life! Create it!

STEP FIVE

Take each element, one at a time, and follow this process. You may decide that, in the time that you have allocated yourself today, you only want to deal with one element, but I would caution you to make notes where what you are capturing spills into another element.

> *"I haven't lived a perfect life.*
> *I have regrets.*
> *But that's from a*
> *lifetime of taking chances,*
> *making decisions,*
> *and trying not to be frozen.*
> *The only thing that I can do with my*
> *regrets is understand them."*
> *Kevin Costner*

Environment – there are many environments in your life: your home, your work space, your hobby space, your meditation space, your exercise space, your car, your garage, your wardrobe, your storage space, your garden, as well as many others.

Using your five senses – look, feel, smell, hearing, and

taste – describe each one of your environments. For example, what size is your home? And for this we aren't specifically talking about how many bedrooms and bathrooms it has, but more about the physical size and layout of each room. While you are thinking about each room and the position of the room in your perfect home, think about the use of each room and things like the furniture that will fill the room. Now that you've thought about the physical space, the location, the use, and what is filling the space; think about colours, emotional feeling, and the smells or aromas. Spilling over into your relationship elements, think about who will be sharing the space with you, or using the space, or coming in and out of the space. Why will they be there? Who are they? What conversations do you have with them? You may ask how taste comes into your environment, but think about the taste of the food you will be cooking in one or more of your spaces - inside or outside.

Once you have created your multiple environments, in your mind's eye walk through each environment. See what you have put into each space. See what colours you have used. Feel the energy of that space as you walk into it, stand/sit in it, and walk out of it. What are you feeling? What emotions? What are you smelling? What are you hearing? What are you saying? Who is with you? Where applicable, what are you tasting? If, as you walk through each environment you notice something that is not right – change it! It maybe something you've added but now don't want. It maybe something in a place that needs to be moved. It maybe something that is missing. Whatever it is, until you walk into, through, and out of each

environment with a feeling that you are in an environment that is entirely without any flaws, defects, or shortcomings; keep designing your environments.

Significant Other – who is this person?

Your significant other may be the person you are living with today – your husband, your wife, your partner, your girl-friend, or your boy-friend – or it may not be.

You can use your five senses here too, but it's important when you are being completely honest with yourself about your significant other that you consider the characterists that are important to you. For example, what colour hair should they have, what colour eyes, how tall, how trustworthy are they, clear communication between you, self-discipline showing an inner calm, their ability to see good, ambition, respect, compassion, realistic, sense of humour, passion, honesty, loyalty, you can count on them always, patience, happy, balance, vulnerable, creative, affectionate, loving, supportive, and the list goes on. It is important that you capture each element of this person in the most infinite detail that you can – the detail that is important to you.

It's easy to create this person because you do truly know what it is you want from your significant other; but it's believing that you can have them, that may be the challenge. Today we are creating your Perfect Life, and if you don't create the individual elements that make up your perfect life, then how can you want to life a Perfect Life?

The more difficult question is 'are you living with this person now?' If not, just acknowledge that and move onto the next step of creating and defining your Perfect Life.

Child/Children – do you want them? Do you have them?

Do you want a child or children in your Perfect Life? It's a simple 'yes' or 'no' answer. If yes, how many? If no, then this element will not be included in your Wheel of Perfect Life.

Extended Family – be clear who they are.

Extended Family isn't something that you can create, but being aware of who they are; you can include or exclude them from your Perfect Life.

Extended Family cover parents, siblings, cousins, grandchildren and so on. Make a list and then note whether that person will be included in your Perfect Life.

Friends – do you want them? Do you have them?

Do you want friends in your Perfect Life? It's a simple 'yes' or 'no' answer. If yes, then this element will be included in your Wheel of Perfect Life and if no, then this element will not be included in your Wheel of Perfect Life.

Make a list of all your friends. Identify your Best Friends, your Close Friends, your Friends, your Acquaintances, and those in your social circle for any other reason. Against each person, note whether that person will be included in your Perfect Life.

Now make a note of the person or people who are missing from your Perfect Life.

Colleagues/Boss – we all have them.

Are they the type of people we want in our Perfect Life? Sometimes it is more difficult to select colleagues and bosses, as you may be in the job that you want, following the career of your Perfect Life; but if you are working with people who don't fit into your ideal, what can you do?

Today it's all about defining who the Perfect Life people are. So take your time and work out who you want your boss to be (if you want one), who you want to be working with, who you want to be working for you, and if applicable, who you want your clients/customers to be.

Finances – are all about the money!

Money comes in and money goes out. It's a normal flow and can be equated to an ocean tide. In your Perfect Life, what money will be coming in? and what will you be expecting to pay out to create, live and maintain your Perfect Life? It's important to know this information, as if you are spending more in creating your Perfect Life than you have in your bank account; at some point the creation will stop.

Be clear about what you need to spend to create each element of your Perfect Life.

Work out what you need to spend to live and maintain each element of your Perfect Life.

Now clarify what money you have coming in, and if this is (1) not coming in from the right place i.e. wrong job, or (2) it is not enough; now is the time to be clear about where the money should be coming from and how much you need.

Health ~ Energy – simply your ability to acquire, convert, allocate, distribute and utilitise the energy you generate sustainably.

The World Health Organisation (WHO) has defined human health as "a state of complete physical, mental, and social well-being and not merely the absence of disease or infirmity."

Health is a single word that defines multiple areas of your well-being. It can include your physical health, your mental health, your well-being; as well as covering areas like relationship health, environmental health, health education, diet, exercise, fitness, as well as disease and coping strategies.

In your Perfect Life how do you see your health? Are you eating well? Are you drinking too much alcohol? Are you keeping fit? Are you doing exercises? Are you thinking clearly? Are you being held back by limiting beliefs? Are your habits stopping you achieving what you want to achieve? Are you positive or are you negative in your outlook to life? Are you in a 'happy state'? May be a little more difficult, but it is important to be clear about your health and energy levels in your Perfect Life.

Holidays – simply a period of time spent away from your normal home environment.

Holidays are usually periods of leisure and recreation, but may also cover time spent away from home helping others i.e. working in a charitable environment building a school.

If holidays are a part of your Perfect Life, what do you want to do on your holidays? Where do you want to go? Who will be with you? How long will you be away from your normal home environment? How will you travel i.e. car, boat, plane? Is the mode of transport personally owned or are you buying a ticket?

If you have a 'generic' Perfect Life holiday, you can now define it; but it would be more beneficial to you to be more specific.

Hobbies – that none income earning activity that brings you satisfaction.

Hobbies are something that you may have started in your youth but have stopped because other 'pressing matters' have taken up your time. Hobbies may also be something that you have found later in life.

Some people consider hobbies to be fishing, dancing, playing cards, archery, astronomy, sports, knitting, crocheting, sewing, gardening, candle making, jewellery making, photography, pottery, quizzes, reading, writing, yoga, going to the gym, swimming, metalwork, model building, rebuilding old cars, trainspotting, Formula 1, and the list is extensive.

Whatever you would like to do with your time, that falls into the definition of a pleasurable activity done outside your work time; now is the time to define it. Be clear about what it is. Be clear about when and how you can do it i.e. if you want to go to a Formula 1 race; which one, when is it and what do you need to do to get there?

Spiritual – relates to your human spirit or soul, rather than to something physical or material.

Not everyone has or wants a spiritual element in their Perfect Life, but if you do; write down:

1. Your definition.
2. What you will be doing to satisfy your spiritual element.
3. Where you will be doing what you want to do.
4. When you will be doing what you want to do.

There may be multiple things that you want to do to incorporate a spiritual element in your Perfect Life and it's important that you capture them all.

Time for ME!

Wow! This is one element of life that is often ignored or forgotten about; but is equally as important as each other element of your life.

Time for Me is sometimes known as Quiet Time, Meditation Time, or Yoga Time; and does focus on time that you spent on yourself, with yourself.

If you want Time for Me in your Perfect Life, you need to include it. It's very easy to consider this as a 'nice to have', but that is not what you are doing now. Right now you are being absolutely and very clear about exactly what living your Perfect Life will look like and feel like. It's imperative that you include every single element with as many details as you can include today.

STEP SIX

In some ways this may be the most difficult step of this exercise.

Take your life as it is today and compare it to your Perfect Life. Simply write down for each element:

- What/Who is in your life today that does not appear in your Perfect Life?
  If this is something that should appear in your Perfect Life, go back and add it in.
- What/Who is not in your life today that appears in your Perfect Life?

This is a time of honesty with yourself. For example, if your current significant other is someone that does not appear in your Perfect Life, you need to include their name.

STEP SEVEN

This exercise may take you hours, days, weeks, or even months; but once you have completed this exercise put your journal away. Let your unconscious mind have time to work through the details.

After a period of time, and only you can determine when you will be ready; take out your journal and reflect what you have written down. Does this still fit with your vision of your Perfect Life?

If the answer is 'no', it is important for you to change that or those elements that do not fit with your vision of your Perfect life.

If the answer is 'yes', now is the time to start creating your Perfect Life.

What if?
What if?
What if?

you could live your Perfect Life?

Tools, Models, Techniques

One of the definitions of Perfect that I read was 'entirely without any flaws, defects, or shortcomings.' Another was 'excellent or complete beyond practical or theoretical improvement.' The definition of life 'a living being, especially a human being.'

What If you could live your life entirely without flaws, defects or shortcomings? What If you could live a life completely beyond any practical or theoretical improvement. What If …?

I was talking to a 'mentor' recently, whose mentoring of junior staff was based around the 'What If' question. A question that opens the mind to opportunities. So while you are looking at the possibility of living your perfect life, answer for yourself only, the following:

What If you could live the life of your dreams?

What if?

What If you were holding onto to a life because you felt an obligation to someone else?

What If that person doesn't have the obligation over you, that you feel?

What If that person wants to live a perfect life but feels an obligation to you?

What If you made a change to the person or people in your life?

What If you let that one person or those people go?

What If you chose who you want in your life? Which person? Which people?

What If you could do the job that you want to do?

What If there was a way to make the change to your career that you want to make?

What If you could have time to spend on your hobbies?

What If you could have time to travel and explore?

What If you had time for socialising?

What If you had time to meditate?

What If you had time to focus on your health?

What If you believed that you could live the life of your dreams?

What If you believed that you were living the life of your dreams?

What If you do define the life of your dreams?

What If you know in your inner most heart what the life of your dreams looks like?

What If you don't define the life of your dreams?

The challenge with the What If question is that it brings to mind a lot of possibilities – What If I can do this? – which is often followed by 'I can't' or 'I don't deserve' or 'what if I hurt someone?' or any other negative question or statement you can think of.

BUT

 you could live the life of your dreams?

Introduction

It's all in the Numbers!

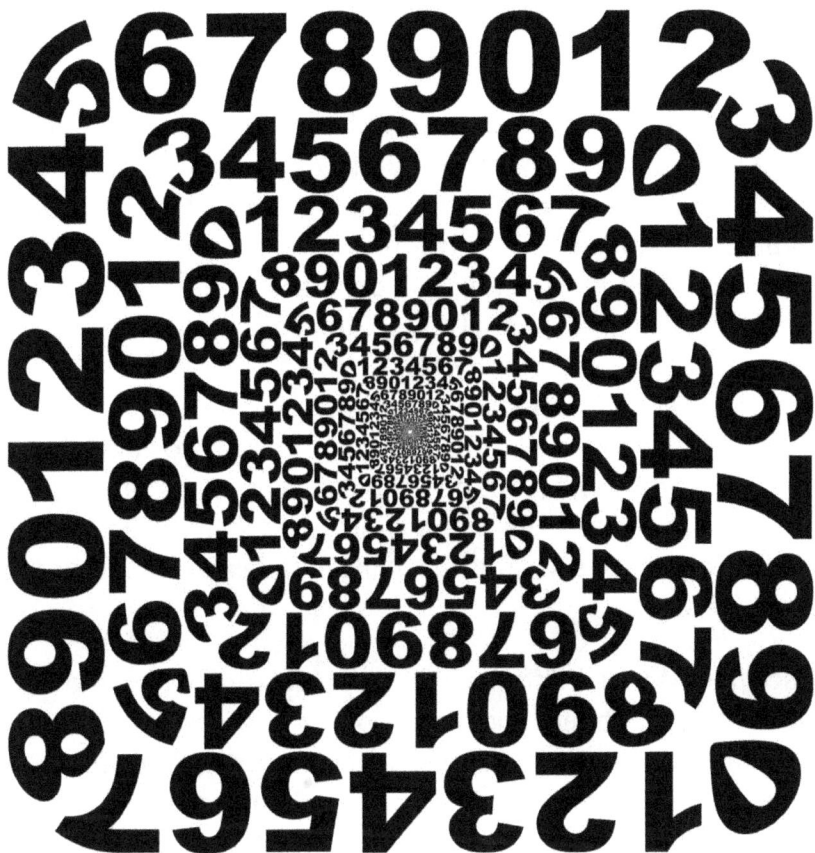

Numerology Series
by
Loren Schmal

For anyone who is interested, curious or even a true believer, the basic definition of numerology is the universal language of numbers. By breaking down the patterns of the universe into numbers, we are able to uncover information about the world as a whole, as well as every individual. Numerology is the science of numbers, but it only involves simple mathematics.

It's more about the personalities of each number, and how each numbers' traits alter the course of your life depending on where they appear in your personal Numerology - if they appear at all. Numerology is a tool used to investigate our own very being, and to bring light our highest potential on the physical, emotional, mental and spiritual planes. Numerology tells of our potential destiny, our natural talents and helps us gain a better understanding of ourselves and others. It shows us the pathway we need to take in our lives to fulfil this potential, and also, tells us one of the many reasons why each one has different traits and characteristics. Numbers have been in existence since the beginning of time and predates all Alphabets.

Each number has a different vibration, and can therefore give us a better understanding of one's pathway, and the circumstances which surround our life. It can direct one to the career best suited to each person, and gives us the opportunity to be more aware of the talents we have and of the pathways we choose to utilize them. It also tells us of the compatibility we have with another, especially who would be most compatible as a partner for you. It tells you how you may best help your family and friends, due to the numbers which control their lives.

Each number is influenced by a different planet in our Solar

System. Each letter of the alphabet vibrates to a given number, 1 – 9, which is also the span of our life cycles. The numbers under which we were born, plus the numbers in our names, are the tools that we are given in order that we may accomplish our mission in life, and enable us to work through all our Karmic Lessons. The Vibratory Power of each number affects us in both Positive and Negative ways.

HOW TO WORK OUT
YOUR OWN NUMEROLOGY

The symbolic meanings that surround the nine whole numbers are the centre of Numerological divination. Numbers are also keyed to letters of the alphabet, so words and names, as well as dates of birth, can be analysed.

Numerology in
Relation to the Alphabet

Each letter of the alphabet is represented by a number between 1 and 9.

1	–	A	J	S
2	–	B	K	T
3	–	C	L	U
4	–	D	M	V
5	–	E	N	W
6	–	F	O	X
7	–	G	P	Y
8	–	H	Q	Z
9	–	I	R	

NAME NUMEROLOGY

The First Name is our 'Foundation in Life'.

To find the total Numerological vibration of your name, translate the letters of your name into the numbers as listed above, and add those number together. Then, break down the result in separate numbers, which you add up again, until you have reduced it to a single digit number. This number is known as your Name Ruling Number.

As an example, let's take the name Chantel. This name translates to C=3, H=8, A=1, N=5, T=2, E=5, L=3.

When we add those numbers (3+8+1+5+2+5+3) we get to 27.

As this is a double digit, which we still need to reduce to 1 digit, we add the numbers of this result.

So: 2+7=9.

The Name Ruling Number for the name Chantel is therefore 9.

DATE OF BIRTH NUMEROLOGY

DAY NUMBER

Your Day Number is the energy which influences who you are and all that you do in your life, on a daily basis. It tells of what makes you respond and act as you do, and is an indication of what type of life you should lead in order to be successful in all that you undertake in this lifetime.

Your Day Number is the day of your birth.

Using as an example the 26th of September 1967, the Day Number is 26 = 2 + 6 = 8.

8 is the Day Number.

DESTINY NUMBER

The destiny number is one of the most important numbers on your chart. It is the ruling force that describes what you must do/learn, in order to operate harmoniously with your environment and how you can get the most out of your present life. It shows the direction you must take, representing the only opportunities for success that will be made available to you.

To analyse and interpret your 'Destiny Number', simply use the formula of reducing your entire date of birth to a single digit.

For example, the 'Destiny Number' for a person with the date of birth of the 26th of September 1967 is 2+6+0+9+1+9+6+7 = 40,
4+0 = 4.

PERSONAL YEAR

The Personal Year Number is the energy by which you will live your life from your birthday of this year, until your birthday of next year. This is the vibration that will influence all that you do throughout that period.

The Personal Year energy is present from birthday to birthday. To work out your Personal Year Number, take the Day and Month Numbers and add them to the Year Number.

For example, the Personal Year Number in 2018 for someone with the date of birth 26/09/1967 would be Number 1. Add the day and month numbers to the year number (2018)
2+6+0+9+2+0+1+8 = 28:
2 + 8 = 10:
1+0=1, making 1 the Personal Year Number.

Loren Schmal
© 2018 Loren Schmal

Founder of CyberPA

It's all in the Numbers!

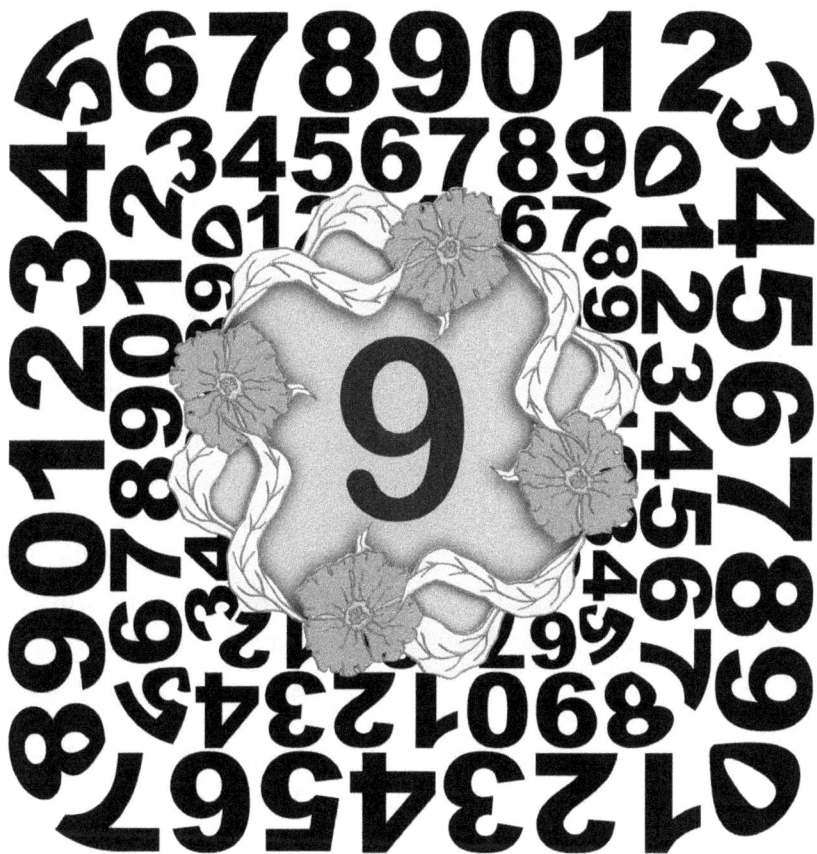

Numerology Series
by
Loren Schmal

The numerology meaning of the number 9
– The Primal Force

Number 9 is the number of universal love, eternity, faith, universal spiritual laws, the concept of karma, spiritual enlightenment, spiritual awakening, service to humanity, humanitarianism and the humanitarian, light working and lightworkers, leading by positive example, philanthropy and the philanthropist, charity, self-sacrifice, selflessness, destiny, life purpose and soul mission, generosity, a higher perspective, romance, inner-strength, public relations, responsibility, intuition, and strength of character.

The number 9 also resonates with learning to say 'No', creative abilities, sensitivity, loyalty, generalist, discretion, brilliance, problem-solving, inner-wisdom, self-love, freedom, popularity, high ideals, tolerance, humility, altruism and benevolence, empathy, non-conformity, artistic genius, an expansive viewpoint, eccentricity, communication, influence, perfection, magnetism, understanding, forgiveness, compassion and sympathy, the visionary, duty and calling, obligation, mysticism, optimism and divine wisdom.

The qualities of the number 9 are those of leadership, the ability to see clearly, integration, the three worlds: physical, intellectual, and spiritual, last symbol before return to unity, ability to understand, inborn talents, compulsions, introspection, personal integrity, unity, truth, the seer, artistry, high moral sense, good advisory, perfection, concord, dissolves ego, attachments, challenges faced in looking for your own wisdom.

Idealistic 9s, capable of realizing those ideals, are intensely passionate people needing to control their wild impulses.

Variously assertive, trusting, generous, selfish and wilful, 9's seriously need stabilizing influences.

In love, 9's are romantic, ardent and impetuous.

What does it mean if you find a Number 9 In your own numbers?

In our Introduction to Numerology we've explained how you can calculate your own numbers. Have any of your numbers turned out to be a 9? If yes, then please find below an explanation as to what this means.

COLOURS associated with number 9

Brown and rich earthy colours are favoured by number 9s, as they are luxuriant colours that reflect confidence and security. They are also soothing colours, that can take the edge off the pressured lives of number 9s. Number 9s also seem to gravitate towards blue and yellow.

9 as a DAY NUMBER

Compassionate, highly intelligent and kind, you are a true humanitarian, a natural teacher, healer and counsellor. The 9 Day person is the natural leader. Within the workplace they will not just do their own jobs, but everyone else's as well. They put their all into getting things done.

The 9 vibration person needs to establish boundaries so that they will not feel depleted by the people in their life.

The 9 Day person may have old family pains that haunt them, and they must work through these emotions in order to be happy today and in the future. You may be inclined to seek an 'alternative' lifestyle.

9 Day Number people make excellent students, and a love of animals is a natural joy to them.

9 Day people sometimes may suffer hardship growing up, and if they had a D or M initial, they may have to cope with financial and/or health issues. If they have a C, L or U initial, they will be very popular.

The 9 can become teachers or vets or do humanitarian work. Many travel a lot and end up living overseas. Those born on the 9th seek alternative lifestyles and make excellent teachers.

Number 9 as Destiny Number

Positive Characteristics:

People born with the Number 9 Destiny are independent, courageous and resilient.

Optimists by nature, number 9s have a happy-go-lucky approach to life and they are more than able to cope with life's ups and downs. Number 9s are sure of themselves and are generally content with their lot.

Once set on a course of action, number 9s will follow their chosen course with determination and they will not be put off or disheartened. Their enthusiasm and vitality can have a positive impact on other people who tend to get carried along with number 9s energies.

Number 9s have hidden depths, as they have a great deal of sympathy and understanding for their fellow human beings. They are non-judgemental of others and are happy to accept people for what and who they are.

Those on the number 9 Life Path are destined to travel a true humanitarian path. They are here to make sacrifices for those less fortunate than themselves and make for an excellent doctor, scientist or charity worker. These sophisticated individuals are very selfless souls and are often patient, trustworthy and honourable, from the very beginning to the end of their lives. They are all about spirituality.

Part of a 9's life path is to express spiritual principles through actions, rather than through preaching or proselytizing.

The karmic responsibility of the 9 on the earth plane is through humanitarian concepts. Your challenge is to let go of material possession and relationships when they have outlived their purposes. Your purpose is to work in any field that benefits mankind.

Negative Characteristics:

A forceful and uncompromising approach to life will get many number 9s where they want to be, but can cause other people great distress. Number 9s do not enjoy conflict or hurting others, and so this aspect of their character needs to be kept in check.

It is important for number 9s to recognize that, unlike themselves, not everyone finds it easy to bounce back from disappointments, and that other people may hurt for a long time after they have moved on.

Quick tempers are common amongst number 9s, as is a tendency to lash out at whoever is nearest.

Number 9s are often guilty of being self-centred and of not listening to others. They have such a belief in themselves that they are not willing to listen to the opinions of others, which can cause resentment.

Number 9 as a PERSONAL YEAR

The 9 Personal Year is one of completion and marks the 'beginning of the ending' of everything you have managed to accomplish during the last decade. This is a year of endings and completion and it is a time to clear out and rid oneself of all that is no longer useful or needed in one's life. De-clutter physically, mentally and emotionally.

It is a year of great changes, though these changes may not be fully recognized at the time.

This is the year you 'reap what you sow'. Whatever you have been working on in the last 9 years will finally pay off. It is a year of squaring old debts and extending forgiveness to all of those to whom you are at cross purposes. There is a strong sense of humanitarian responsibility, tolerance and improved understanding present during this year.

This is an uncomfortable year for many individuals, especially if they are unable to embrace change. You may feel restless and things that used to interest you may be replaced by new desires. If you are not able to let go of the past willingly, a situation may manifest that forces you to change. Success and happiness come in this year through being emotionally detached and letting go of whatever starts to leave one's life. There will be some loss through this year. Clear your space for new beginnings. De-clutter physically, mentally and emotionally and resolve old family issues.

The 9 Personal Year is a cleansing year, between the end of one cycle and the beginning of the next. It is also a time for metaphysical studies and writing. It is a year that is suited to travel, especially for long journeys, and is also a year to make new and exciting friendships, and the termination of old relationships that are no longer necessary in one's life.

Manifesting peace and harmony in all aspects of your life is possible, and is a key to your personal happiness, throughout this year and into the future.

The 9 Personal Year invites you to pay special attention to your inner world. You have graduated from a cycle of experience and it is a time for completing many areas of experience so that you can move freely into the next cycle ahead, without carrying forward outgrown or unneeded baggage. There is a letting go of the old as anticipation of future possibilities exists within you. Gratefulness and compassion are especially important at this time.

Number 9 in CAREER

Minister, Reverend, occultist, metaphysician, literary field, designer, nursing, social worker, body worker, holistic health, composer, teacher, scientist, actor, artist, craftsperson, painter, architect, counsellor or diplomat, world/community leader.

Loren Schmal
© 2018 Loren Schmal

Founder of CyberPA

One of the secrets to creating your Perfect Life is as much about what you give up, as the steps you take to create your Perfect Life.

- Are you willing to make the change or changes that you need to make to create and move into your Perfect Life?
- Are you willing to ignore the comments people will make, when you let them know about the changes you want to make?
- Are you will to give up things that you don't want in your Perfect Life?
- What are you willing to give up, to create and move into living your Perfect Life?

"Are you willing to live as other people won't, so maybe you can live as other people can't."
Mastin Kipp

What you focus on, is what you create; but how? Follow these points to help you identify and work through what you need to give up, to create your Perfect Life:

1. **Excuses**
   Are you willing to stop making excuses?
   We often find excuses when things feel a little tough. Either you want to change your life, or you don't; but if you really do want to change your life, part of what you need to give up to move forward, is giving up excuses that justify you not making the changes that you need to make. Believing your excuses gives them a validity, which will only temporarily make you feel better about your reasons for not making the changes you need to make to live your Perfect Life. Either you do want to live the Perfect Life, or you don't. Whichever it is, be honest with

yourself, rather than make excuses.

2. **Time**
   Are you willing to make time?
   Time is one thing that you often don't have enough of. Your life is busy. Now that you've made the decision to define and create your Perfect Life, how do you find the time to take the steps to create your Perfect Life? Each step will take time. What do you need to give up, to be able to make the time?

3. **The Fear of Failure**
   Are you willing to break through your fear of failure?
   Your fear of failure will hold you back. Believing in your fear, will leave you unwilling to take chances; it will leave you in situations that you want to change; it will stop you changing your relationships; it will stop you changing your circumstances; it will just stop you. It is your life and only you can stop yourself. What are you willing to do, to break through your fears, your fear of failure?

4. **The Fear of Uncertainty**
   Are you willing to believe that you can certainly live your Perfect Life?
   It is said that nothing in life is certain; that there are no guarantees. But changing your life, to allow you to live your Perfect Life, does not mean that you are moving away from the path of current certainty and into the path of a life of the future unknown. Believing that your life cannot be changed, that being uncertain about your future is a bad thing, will hold you back from making the changes that you need to make to live your Perfect Life. Are you willing to believe that you can life your Perfect Life?

5. **Learned Helplessness**

   Are you willing to learn anything and everything that you need to do, to change your life for your Perfect Life?

   Sometimes when you are in a position where you have faced so many challenges to get where you are in your life today, you may begin to feel powerless to face new challenges yet again. Feeling helpless, feeling that you can't learn anything else, will hold you in the life that you are in today. The feeling of being overwhelmed about what you've learnt so far, can stop you from wanting to learn anything else.

   Learning now that you are the only person in control of your life, will help you understand that you and only you can learn what you need to learn to make those changes. What do you need to do, to stop yourself from giving up on the opportunity to live your Perfect Life?

6. **Ignoring … Resisting … Feelings … Discomfort**

   Are you willing to do anything that you need to do, to live your Perfect Life?

   As you look at your life today, and you look at what you want your life to be; are you now feeling powerless? It is very easy to take one step back, ignore what you've defined as your Perfect Life, and stay in the life that you have today.

   It is very easy to pretend that the life that you are living today is your Perfect Life. Just ignore that what you know is the life you want to live. Would you rather stick your head in the sand and pretend that everything is OK?

   Stepping outside your own comfort zone is uncomfortable. Often, it's easier to continue to do what you are doing now; it makes you feel more at ease; it helps you to avoid the inevitable feelings of discomfort.

   Only you can make the decision to make the changes.

Only you can design your Perfect Life. Only you can work out what needs to be removed from your life today. Only you can work out what you need to add to your life today. Only YOU … !

What are you willing to do,
- to step out of your comfort zone;
- to resist starting and making those changes;
- to ignore you feelings of powerless, fear and concern;
- to pretend that you are living the Perfect Life now, when you know that you aren't;
- to be honest about the problems in your life today, that you know you can change;
- to move through your discomfort into a place of joy and happiness in your new Perfect Life;

What are you willing to do to live your own Perfect Life?

7. **Beliefs and Habits**

   Are you willing to challenge your limiting beliefs and negative habits?

   Limiting beliefs are simply those things in your unconscious mind that stop you from doing something. It's the 'thing' that automatically says 'no', when if you stopped and truly listened, you would probably say 'yes'. Limiting beliefs can be changed by becoming aware of them. What are they. How do they impact on your day-to-day decisions? How do they stop you from doing what you need to do, to make the changes that you need to make? When you know what they are, write them in your journal and immediately change the 'no' to a 'yes', the 'negative' to a 'positive'. For example, instead of saying 'no I won't be climbing Kilimanjaro', say 'yes, but I am not sure when I will climb Kilimanjaro'. That gives you the chance to investigate and learn before you take action and actually climb Kilimanjaro.

Habits come from your formative years and your beliefs; and is defined as a regular behaviour that is repeated unconsciously. It's often the habit to say 'no' which creates and supports the limiting belief of 'no'. Becoming aware of the times you automatically do something that doesn't help you change your life, is the way to make the change.

Are you willing to change your limiting beliefs and negative habits into positive beliefs and habits?

8. **Envy ... Waiting ... Procrastination**
   Are you willing to stop envying others, stop waiting for things to 'just happen' and stop procrastinating?

   It is very easy to envy other people who have what you want in your Perfect Life, but what if this sets you up for self-sabotage. 'Because they have it, doesn't mean I'm worthy of having the same?'

   What happens if you wait until you 'feel like' starting? It's often easier to procrastinate and wait until you feel like doing something, but it's your life that you want to change and until you start the process to change – nothing will!

   It simple to wait until someone else makes a move before you do. If one of the things that you need to do, is to change one or more of your personal or professional relationships, you can chose from two options – (1) you make the change or (2) you wait for them to make the change.

   The reality is that, unless you take that first step, nothing will change. You will continue to live the life you are living today. You will not move into and live the life that you've defined as your Perfect Life.

   Are you willing to change your habits to be more action proactive?

9. **What do you need to GIVE UP?**

Are you willing to give up those things that are not a part of your new Perfect Life?

Which relationships do you need to give up?

What do you need to give up in your career or business?

Which hobbies do you need to give up?

What do you need to give up in terms of improving your health?

What do you need to give up to take the holidays you dream of taking?

What do you need to give up to live in the environment you dream of living in?

What do you need to give up in order to improve your financial situation?

What do you need to change so that you give up trying to do everything yourself?

What habits do you need to give up in order to move into living your Perfect Life?

What limiting beliefs do you need to give up in order to move into living your Perfect Life?

What do you need to give up in order to make the changes you want to make, in order to live your Perfect Life?

Are you willing to make the changes you need to make, so that you can life your Perfect Life?

"Maybe life isn't about avoiding the bruises.
Maybe it's about collecting the scars,
to prove we showed up for it."
Unknown

Each point above starts and ends with a question that gives you the opportunity to answer 'yes' or 'no'. If you select to answer 'yes', then you know that you are willing to give up, whatever it is that you need to give up, to make the changes you want to make, to live YOUR PERFECT LIFE!

If you have answered 'no' to one or more of the questions, then ask yourself the following questions:

What would happen if you said 'yes' and did make the change?

> What would happen if you said 'yes' and didn't make the change?

> What would not happen if you said 'yes' and did make the change?

> What would not happen if you said 'yes' and didn't make the change?

There is only one life to live and only one person to make the decisions on how to live that life. You know, in your mind's eye, in your inner most heart, what your Perfect Life looks like and feels like; and only you can make the decision about how you spend your time – staying where you are today? or moving forward and living your Perfect Life?

Where do I start?

Dear Amarantine Team,

As I am 45 years old, and my last child is due to leave home to attend university after summer, I am going through this struggle of making up the balance of my life.

I'm sure this phase must be the so called empty-nest syndrome, and I know that this experience is very normal to go through. But that doesn't really help! I feel like I have put my own life and career on hold as I was raising my children. The children have always come first, and that is reflected in almost every aspect of my life today. I am living in a completely run-down home, I look (and feel) like a mom who has always paid more attention to her children's appearance then her own, I work in a crappy job because all I wanted was to pay the bills and to be able to work flexible hours, and I don't really have a personal life as I never had time to create one. And that was all fine as long as I had my children running around and needing my care and assistance.

But now, with an empty house in sight, my life is looking really empty as well.

I already know what I would like my perfect life to look like in 5 years from now, but as almost every aspect of my life needs change, I have no clue where to start and I feel completely overwhelmed! What should I do?

Penelope Cassidy, London, United Kingdom

Dear Penelope,

This issue of Amarantine provided you with the "Perfect Wheel of Life" as a tool to help you construct your perfect life. Usually, coaches will suggest to pick the 2 or 3 elements most important to you, in order to make a start.

However, when reading your letter, I would suggest a slightly different approach. You know you want to make changes, but you feel overwhelmed with the majority of them. And in the meantime, reading in between the lines, you don't seem to feel that happy.

Therefore, instead of focusing on the most important elements of your life which need change, I would suggest that you focus on "quick wins" first. Which changes can you make relatively quickly, to help you make an initial start with turning your life around? Maybe you can start by clearing out the house, and giving it a fresh paint? Maybe you can start by visiting a hairdresser and a shopping spree, to make you feel a bit better about your appearance? Maybe you can join a class or hobby group, to help create some personal time? Maybe you can focus on finding a new job? Maybe you can...

I am confident that you will find that, when making even the tiniest changes, you'll start to feel better. Better about your life, better about yourself, and better about your future. And that will inspire you and boost you with positive energy to make more changes, and also tackle the bigger changes as you move on. I hope that this issue of Amarantine will inspire you to take control and start making those changes!

Warmest regards,
The Amarantine Team

NEW YORK TIMES BESTSELLER

LASTING HAPPINESS IN A CHANGING WORLD

The Book of
JOY

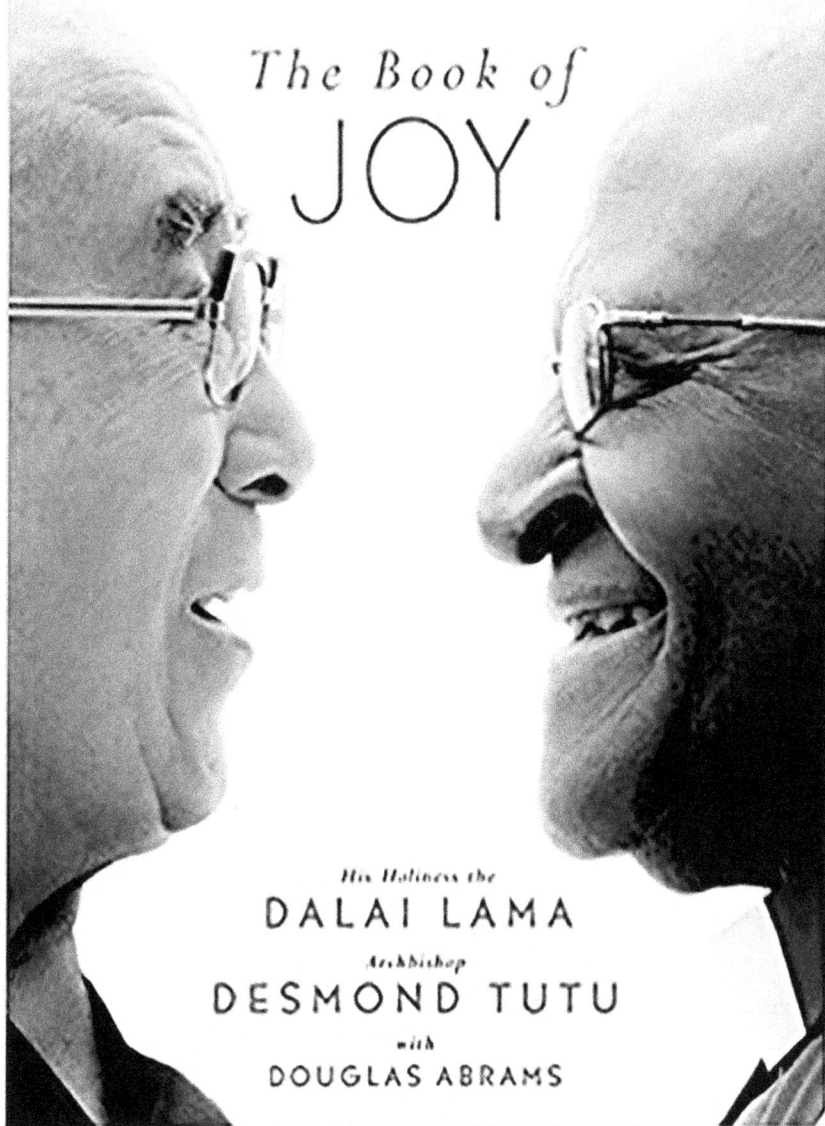

His Holiness the
DALAI LAMA
Archbishop
DESMOND TUTU
with
DOUGLAS ABRAMS

Welcome to your Personal & Professional Development with Amarantine

Amarantine supports your Personal and Professional Development through assessing, exploring, developing, and inspiring yourself to increase your self-awareness, self-knowledge, self-confidence, and self-esteem; to help you identify and develop your talents, skills, knowledge, competence, and experience to fulfil your personal aspirations in both your personal and professional life, to provide you with an enhanced lifestyle and improved quality of life as a result.

Whether you have a personal goal or a professional career goal, Amarantine will answer the questions you ask in an inspirational manner that helps you take the next step to achieve your own personal and professional aspirations.

Amarantine supports lifelong learning; which is achieved through both formal and informal learning processes. Formal learning is defined as education and training; whereas informal learning comes from coaching, mentoring, supervision, as well as things you experience, see, and hear in your everyday life.

Amarantine will inspire you to consciously learn and develop in all areas of your personal and professional life.

www.Amarantine.Life